Logistics 2040: Navigating the Future of Supply Chain Management

Oswald Sanon

DEDICATION

To the countless men and women serving in the logistics and supply chain sectors, whose tireless efforts ensure that the world keeps moving, even in the most challenging of times. To my colleagues and mentors in the military, who taught me the value of precision, efficiency, and adaptability, lessons that have shaped my view of the future.

And to the next generation of supply chain professionals, who will navigate the complexities of a rapidly changing world, may this book serve as a compass guiding you toward innovation, resilience, and success.

CONTENTS

Introduction

INTRODUCTION

Supply chain management and logistics, twin engines propelling the global economy, have deep historical roots dating back to ancient times when trade routes were first established. Over the centuries, these systems have evolved from simple barter trade routes to complex global networks. The turn of the 21st century marked the beginning of rapid advancements in technology and an acceleration in globalization that spurred unprecedented complexity and scale in logistics and supply chain management.

In the present day, the logistics and supply chain industry is a dynamic and vital component of the global economy. It's an industry characterized by intricate networks, multi-tiered linkages, and interdependencies that span across continents. It encompasses a wide range of activities, from procurement of raw materials to delivery of finished goods to the end consumer, and all the processes in between. We are currently in an era of rapid transformation, shaped by digitization, advanced analytics, and shifting consumer demands. The COVID-19 pandemic has further amplified the importance of resilient and agile supply chains, revealing both vulnerabilities and opportunities for improvement.

"Logistics 2040: Navigating the Future of Supply Chain Management" is envisioned as a navigational tool for this rapidly evolving landscape. This book aims to look forward into the future of the industry, exploring emerging trends, technologies, and strategies that are poised to reshape the world of supply chain and logistics. As much as it is about technology and advanced models, it is also about people, the environment, and the global economy.

Each chapter of this book delves into a specific aspect of the future of logistics and supply chain. We will explore how technologies like AI, machine learning, and blockchain are revolutionizing supply chain processes, how data analytics is driving efficient decision-making, and the role of sustainability in the supply chain strategies of the future. We will discuss the evolution of the human factor, the resilience of supply chains, and the impact of global trade regulations. Further chapters will investigate the future of logistics, the influence of e-commerce, advances in material handling, implications of the Fourth Industrial Revolution, and many more pertinent topics.

The aim of this book is not to predict the future with absolute certainty – for no one can – but rather to prepare for it by understanding potential trends and being ready to adapt. We will learn from real-world case studies and hear from experts at the forefront of supply chain innovation.

Our journey begins here, and like every successful supply chain, it requires collaboration, agility, and a willingness to adapt to the ever-changing landscape. Whether you are a seasoned professional, a student of supply chain management, or an interested outsider, this book offers insights that will broaden your understanding of the field and inspire you to participate in shaping its future. Welcome to "Logistics 2040: Navigating the Future of Supply Chain Management."

CHAPTER 1
TECHNOLOGY AND THE SUPPLY CHAIN

In today's connected world, technology plays an integral role in shaping the future of industries. One such industry witnessing the tremendous impact of technological innovation is supply chain and logistics. The proliferation of digital transformation, Artificial Intelligence (AI), Machine Learning (ML), blockchain technology, Internet of Things (IoT), and Augmented Reality (AR) & Virtual Reality (VR) technologies are reshaping the modus operandi of supply chains.

The digital transformation in supply chains and logistics has blurred the lines between the physical and digital world. At the heart of this transformation is the movement of data. Data has become the "new oil," driving efficiencies and innovations. Consider Amazon's e-commerce operations. The retail giant uses sophisticated algorithms to predict demand, optimize inventory, and deliver goods faster than ever. This is digital transformation at its finest – using digital technology to drive significant improvements in performance and expand the customer base.

Artificial Intelligence and Machine Learning are proving to be game changers for supply chains. AI algorithms are used to predict demand, optimize routes, manage inventory, and even automate customer service through chatbots. Machine learning models learn from data patterns to make predictions or decisions without being explicitly programmed. For example, IBM's Watson AI has been used in supply chain scenarios to predict disruptions and mitigate risks.

The rise of blockchain technology is another critical development, particularly for track-and-trace in supply chains. With its decentralized and immutable characteristics, blockchain provides transparency and traceability, two essential elements in today's complex supply chains. It can accurately track a product's journey from raw material to finished good, providing assurance of origin and authenticity. A case in point is De Beers' diamond blockchain initiative, which ensures the diamonds are conflict-free, and their journey can be traced from mine to retailer.

The Internet of Things is enabling real-time monitoring and decision-making in supply chains. Sensors on products, vehicles, and machines provide a constant stream of data, allowing companies to track goods in real time and make data-driven decisions. For instance, DHL uses IoT for operational efficiency in its warehouses. Sensors on forklifts monitor the vehicles' usage and ensure they are utilized effectively, resulting in significant cost savings.

Lastly, Augmented Reality (AR) and Virtual Reality (VR) are finding their way into training and warehouse operations. AR can assist workers in picking operations, guiding them to the correct items and quantities, improving accuracy and productivity. VR is used in training, providing a safe and controlled environment for learning new tasks or understanding complex situations. Walmart, for example, uses VR to train its employees on handling Black Friday rush.

All these technologies are driving a more connected, transparent, and efficient supply chain. But these are still early days, and there is much more to come. As we move deeper into this century, we will witness even more exciting technological innovations that will redefine how we manage and operate supply chains.

Just as the ancient mariners used the stars and compass to navigate the vast oceans, the modern supply chain professionals will use these technologies as navigational tools in the vast complexity of global supply chains. As we proceed to the next chapter, we delve deeper into the power of data in supply chains, the lifeblood that gives these technologies their transformative capabilities.

As we look towards 2040, we can expect these technologies to become more deeply ingrained in supply chain operations. They have the potential to greatly improve efficiency and accuracy, while also making training safer and more effective.

In the following chapters, we will dive deeper into each of these technologies, exploring their potential and considering the challenges they may pose. We will examine case studies, hear from experts in the field, and contemplate what the world of logistics and supply chain might look like in 2040. As we continue this journey, it's important to remember that technology is not an end in itself, but a tool that, when used wisely, can lead to unprecedented levels of efficiency, accuracy, and customer satisfaction in the   supply   chain.

CHAPTER 2
THE POWER OF DATA

The power of data in the world of logistics and supply chain management cannot be overstated. With advances in technology and digital transformation, we're witnessing an exponential increase in data being generated every moment. This "Big Data," characterized by its volume, velocity, and variety, offers immense possibilities and is becoming the cornerstone of modern supply chain management.

The role of big data in predictive analysis and decision making is transformative. In the past, supply chain management was largely reactive, with organizations responding to events and issues as they arose. Now, with big data analytics, companies can predict future trends and demand patterns, providing the ability to be proactive. For example, an organization can analyze past sales data, combined with external factors like market trends, economic indicators, and even weather patterns, to accurately forecast future demand. This predictive capability leads to better inventory management, reduced costs, and improved customer service.

The emergence of real-time analytics is taking big data a step further. By analyzing data in real-time, organizations can make immediate decisions that enhance supply chain efficiency and customer experience. For instance, real-time tracking of delivery vehicles allows logistics companies to reroute their drivers on-the-fly based on current traffic conditions, thereby reducing delivery times.

Data-driven supply chain optimization is the end-goal. By harnessing the power of data, companies can optimize all elements of the supply chain, from procurement to production, warehousing, transportation, and final delivery. An optimized supply chain is characterized by reduced costs, increased efficiency, improved customer service, and greater agility to respond to market changes.

Now let's consider some real-world case studies of companies that have successfully leveraged data.

One such example is Starbucks. The coffee giant collects and analyzes enormous amounts of data from its 30,000 stores worldwide to optimize various aspects of its supply chain. By analyzing data points such as customer preferences, buying habits, and seasonal demand, Starbucks can predict future trends, manage inventory more efficiently, and provide a superior customer experience.

Another example is UPS, the world's largest package delivery company. UPS uses big data analytics to optimize its delivery routes, a system they call ORION (On-Road Integrated Optimization and Navigation). ORION analyzes a multitude of data, including package delivery information, vehicle telematics, and map data, to provide drivers with optimized routes. This has reportedly saved UPS over 100 million miles driven per year, significantly reducing costs and environmental impact.

As we navigate deeper into the world of "Logistics 2040," it becomes evident that the ability to harness the power of data is a critical competency for any organization. As we move forward, the successful organizations will be those that can turn their data into actionable insights to drive decision-making and enhance supply chain performance. The next chapter will take us into the realm of sustainability, another vital aspect of future supply chains and an area where data-driven decision making can make a significant   impact.

CHAPTER 3
SUSTAINABILITY IN THE SUPPLY CHAIN

As we delve further into the exploration of supply chain management's future, one theme that is taking center stage globally is sustainability. The growing environmental and social consciousness amongst consumers, along with regulatory pressures, has compelled businesses to seek sustainable practices in their supply chain operations.

The importance of eco-friendly and sustainable practices cannot be overstated in today's world. Climate change, resource depletion, and growing inequalities are significant challenges that humanity faces. The supply chain, with its global reach and resource-intensive nature, has a crucial role to play in addressing these challenges. Eco-friendly practices in supply chains can range from reducing emissions in transportation, optimizing packaging to minimize waste, sourcing from suppliers with sustainable practices, to even designing products with end-of-life recycling in mind.

This push for sustainability has led to a shift towards circular supply chains. Unlike traditional linear models ('take-make-waste'), circular supply chains aim to design out waste and pollution, keep products and materials in use, and regenerate natural systems. It's a system where the output is returned back into the system as an input for future production, creating a closed-loop, circular system.

Green logistics is an integral part of sustainable supply chains. It focuses on reducing environmental impact across logistics activities, including transportation, and packaging. The benefits are twofold: not only does it contribute to environmental preservation, but it also can result in cost savings through efficient use of resources.

The role of technology in promoting sustainability is significant. Technologies such as big data and AI can optimize routes and loads to reduce fuel consumption in transportation. IoT sensors can monitor energy usage in warehouses and help implement energy-saving measures. Blockchain can ensure transparency in sourcing, ensuring that materials are responsibly sourced.

Several companies serve as excellent case studies of sustainability in supply chains. Patagonia, an outdoor apparel company, is renowned for its commitment to sustainability. It has implemented a "Worn Wear" program, encouraging customers to trade-in their used Patagonia clothing for credits. These used clothes are cleaned, repaired, and resold, effectively creating a circular supply chain.

IKEA is another such example. The company is striving to become 'climate positive' by 2030. It plans to achieve this by designing products with end-of-life recycling in mind, sourcing materials from sustainable sources, and optimizing its logistics operations to reduce emissions.

As we move forward into "Logistics 2040," it becomes clear that sustainability is not just an option but a necessity for supply chains. The next chapter will delve into the evolving role of humans in this increasingly automated and data-driven landscape. The intersection of technology, data, and human capital is where the future of supply chain management will be shape.

CHAPTER 4
THE HUMAN FACTOR

As we delve deeper into the future of supply chain management, a central element to consider is the human factor. As much as technology and automation play pivotal roles in the evolution of supply chains, it's humans who create, control, and innovate these systems. Amid rapid automation and digital transformation, the role of humans in the supply chain is not diminishing; instead, it is evolving.

Automation and Artificial Intelligence (AI) have significantly impacted supply chain operations, promising efficiency, speed, and accuracy beyond human capabilities. Robots are performing tasks in warehouses, and algorithms are making decisions based on vast amounts of data. However, this doesn't spell the end for human involvement; instead, it calls for a shift in the type of tasks humans perform. Humans are needed to design, implement, monitor, and improve these automated systems. More significantly, humans bring creativity, strategic thinking, and problem-solving skills that no algorithm can match.

The transition towards a more automated supply chain presents both a challenge and an opportunity for the workforce. The challenge lies in the potential displacement of workers performing tasks that are being automated. The opportunity, however, is the creation of new roles that require skills in managing and improving automated systems.

This leads to the importance of upskilling and retraining the workforce for the future. As technology evolves, so too must the skills of the workforce. Companies must invest in continuous learning programs, providing their employees with opportunities to learn new skills relevant to the evolving landscape. This could range from technical skills such as data analysis or programming, to softer skills like problem-solving, strategic thinking, and change management.

Leadership plays a crucial role in this transformation. Leaders must not only envision the future but also guide their organizations through the change. They need to foster a culture that embraces innovation, encourages learning, and is not afraid to take calculated risks. This culture forms the bedrock upon which successful innovation thrives.

Several companies serve as great examples of how humans and machines can work together synergistically. Amazon, with its automated warehouses, also employs thousands of people to oversee the operations, solve problems, and continually improve the system. At the same time, Amazon invests heavily in training programs for its employees, preparing them for the future.

Another example is Toyota, known for its 'Toyota Production System' that heavily relies on the concept of continuous improvement ('Kaizen'). While Toyota uses automation in its production, it emphasizes the role of humans in identifying problems, innovating, and improving the system.

As we move into "Logistics 2040," the interplay between technology and the human factor will continue to shape the future of supply chains. While machines bring efficiency and accuracy, it's the human element that brings creativity, flexibility, and strategic thinking. The next chapter will explore how these, along with technology and data, contribute to building supply chain   resilience.

CHAPTER 5
SUPPLY CHAIN RESILIENCE

As we navigate the ever-evolving world of supply chains, resilience has emerged as a crucial element of successful operations. The importance of building a resilient supply chain has been underscored by past disruptions, with the COVID-19 pandemic serving as a significant, recent example.

COVID-19 blindsided the world and its impact reverberated throughout global supply chains. Manufacturing hubs were shut down, consumer demand patterns altered radically, and logistics faced numerous challenges from restrictions and safety concerns. The pandemic revealed vulnerabilities in supply chains worldwide, as many struggled with shortages, delays, and escalating costs.

However, it also provided valuable lessons. The most significant is perhaps the inherent risk in concentrating production in specific geographical areas, a practice popularized by economic considerations and efficiencies of scale. The disruption of these hubs caused ripple effects down the supply chain, affecting businesses and consumers worldwide. Another lesson was the importance of adaptability. Supply chains that could swiftly adjust their strategies and operations to accommodate changing circumstances fared better than those that could not.

These lessons feed into the strategies for building a resilient supply chain. Firstly, diversification is crucial. Depending on a single source or location for production is risky; having alternatives allows for flexibility in times of disruption. Secondly, maintaining adequate safety stock can cushion against sudden demand or supply fluctuations. However, this must be balanced with the costs of carrying extra inventory.

The digitization of supply chain operations enhances resilience by providing real-time visibility and enabling swift decision-making. Supply chain visibility - the ability to track and monitor supply chain activities in real-time - allows for rapid identification and response to disruptions. It's the difference between reacting to a problem after it has occurred and proactively managing issues before they escalate.

Agility, the ability to respond to changes quickly and efficiently, is another cornerstone of a resilient supply chain. This involves flexible manufacturing processes, dynamic logistics operations, and a workforce ready to adapt to changing circumstances. The use of AI and predictive analytics, as discussed in previous chapters, can significantly enhance supply chain agility by providing foresight and enabling preemptive actions.

Several companies exemplify resilience in their supply chains. For instance, during the COVID-19 pandemic, companies like Unilever and Nestle demonstrated resilience by rapidly adjusting their manufacturing processes, diversifying their supplier base, and using data analytics to forecast changing consumer patterns and manage their inventory accordingly.

As we progress towards "Logistics 2040," building resilience will continue to be a top priority for supply chains. It's not just about surviving disruptions but emerging stronger and more efficient in the face of them. Future chapters will delve into other aspects influencing supply chain resilience, such as regulatory environments, global trade dynamics, and advances in technology.

CHAPTER 6
REGULATORY ENVIRONMENT AND GLOBAL TRADE

As we move deeper into the world of "Logistics 2040," it is imperative to delve into the complexities of the regulatory environment and the broader landscape of international trade. Supply chains are inherently global, linking raw material suppliers, manufacturers, and customers across multiple jurisdictions. As such, they are influenced by various international trade agreements, regulations, and compliance requirements.

Trade agreements directly affect international supply chains. These pacts, made between two or more nations, define the terms of trade between them, including tariffs, import and export regulations, and standards. For example, the North American Free Trade Agreement (NAFTA) and its successor, the United States-Mexico-Canada Agreement (USMCA), have significantly shaped supply chains in North America by reducing trade barriers and facilitating cross-border movement of goods.

However, these agreements can also pose challenges. Changes to existing agreements or the introduction of new ones can disrupt established supply chains. The recent shift from NAFTA to USMCA exemplifies this, requiring companies to adapt to new rules and regulations. Furthermore, trade tensions, such as those between the U.S. and China, can create uncertainty and instability, making long-term planning difficult for businesses.

In the digital age, compliance and regulatory requirements have expanded beyond physical goods and tariffs. Digital trade, data privacy, and cybersecurity are now integral components of global trade and regulation. The General Data Protection Regulation (GDPR) in the European Union and the California Consumer Privacy Act (CCPA) in the U.S. are examples of new regulations that supply chain operators must understand and comply with.

Non-compliance with these rules can result in hefty penalties, reputational damage, and in some cases, revocation of the license to operate in certain markets. Moreover, regulations vary across jurisdictions, making compliance a complex task for global supply chains. Technology can play a crucial role here, with solutions like AI and blockchain offering potential ways to monitor and manage regulatory compliance across different regions.

Operating in the global supply chain involves both risks and opportunities. Political instability, fluctuating exchange rates, and natural disasters are key risks that can disrupt operations. However, global supply chains also offer the chance to tap into new markets, access diverse talent pools, and benefit from economies of scale. The key lies in striking a balance: leveraging opportunities while mitigating risks through diversification, robust risk management practices, and the strategic use of technology.

Take the example of Apple. The tech giant's supply chain extends over 43 countries and involves hundreds of suppliers. This global presence allows Apple to leverage different markets' benefits, access diverse talent, and maintain its status as a leader in the industry. However, it also means dealing with complex regulatory frameworks, managing geopolitical risks, and adhering to varied trade agreements.

Navigating the complexities of global trade and regulations is integral to operating successful, resilient supply chains. As we head towards "Logistics 2040," businesses will need to keep abreast of evolving trade agreements, regulatory changes, and global market dynamics. They will need to leverage technology and data to ensure compliance, manage risks, and seize opportunities in the vast, interconnected world of global supply chains.

CHAPTER 7
THE FUTURE OF LOGISTICS

The future of logistics is unfolding before our eyes, shaped by technological advancements and evolving consumer demands. This chapter delves into the emerging trends and innovations that are set to reshape warehousing, transportation, and delivery models in the coming years.

Warehousing and transportation form the backbone of logistics. As we move towards 2040, these sectors will experience substantial transformations. Smart warehouses, where technology is integrated at every level, are becoming more common. IoT sensors can track inventory in real-time, while AI and ML can analyze this data to improve operations. Autonomous robots, guided by computer vision and machine learning, can efficiently pick and pack items, reducing human error and increasing speed.

Transportation is also experiencing its fair share of innovation. Autonomous vehicles are already being tested in various logistics applications, with the promise of reducing labor costs and increasing safety. Drones, too, are poised to revolutionize delivery, especially in remote or densely populated areas where traditional delivery methods struggle.

The concept of "last mile" delivery, referring to the final step in the delivery process from a distribution center to the end user, has been a challenging aspect of supply chain management. However, new technologies and innovative solutions are poised to disrupt this domain. Micro-fulfillment centers, situated within cities close to consumers, can enable faster deliveries. Similarly, the use of lockers where consumers can pick up their packages at their convenience is gaining popularity. New delivery modes, such as drones and robots, are also being explored for their potential in last-mile delivery.

As logistics evolves, we're also seeing a significant shift towards customer-centric supply chains. Customers are no longer passive recipients at the end of the supply chain; instead, they are active participants influencing its design and operations. Demand for personalization, ethical sourcing, and sustainable practices are shaping how products are produced, transported, and delivered.

Finally, third-party logistics (3PLs) and fourth-party logistics (4PLs) providers will play an increasingly important role in the future of logistics. 3PLs, companies that provide multiple logistics services, are likely to expand their offerings and invest in advanced technologies to meet their customers' evolving needs. 4PLs, or 'lead logistics providers', manage other 3PLs, integrating all aspects of the supply chain. Their role is set to become more strategic, focusing on data analysis, network optimization, and providing end-to-end supply chain solutions.

Consider the case of Amazon. The e-commerce giant continues to push the boundaries of logistics innovation, from its automated warehouses to its investments in drone delivery and its move into becoming a 3PL itself through "Amazon Shipping." These initiatives show how companies can leverage technologies and innovative models to transform their logistics operations.

As we look towards "Logistics 2040," we see a future characterized by digitization, automation, and a focus on the customer. This transformation will not be easy; it will require investment, adaptability, and a commitment to continuous innovation. However, the potential rewards in terms of efficiency, cost savings, and customer satisfaction make this journey worth undertaking.

CHAPTER 8
THE ROLE OF E-COMMERCE

As we look forward to the future of supply chain management and logistics, we cannot ignore the profound influence of e-commerce. Its growth is not just a trend, but a tectonic shift in how consumers shop and how businesses operate. This chapter aims to explore the rise of e-commerce, its impact on the supply chain, the shift towards omni-channel retailing, and evolving fulfillment strategies.

E-commerce has grown exponentially in the past decade. Consumers value the convenience, variety, and pricing transparency that online shopping offers. Businesses, on the other hand, see e-commerce to reach a global customer base, launch new products quickly, and gather valuable consumer insights. This growth in e-commerce has significant implications for supply chain management and logistics, transforming how goods are stored, packed, shipped, and delivered.

One significant trend emerging from the rise of e-commerce is the shift towards omni-channel retailing. Omni-channel retailing involves providing customers with a seamless shopping experience across physical stores and digital platforms (e-commerce sites, mobile apps, social media). This integrated approach requires a supply chain that can efficiently manage and link multiple sales channels, maintain consistent inventory levels, and provide a seamless customer experience.

However, omni-channel retailing presents its unique challenges. Maintaining consistency across different channels, managing returns, and meeting consumer expectations for fast, reliable delivery are all considerable tasks. With customers expecting the same level of service regardless of where they choose to shop, supply chains must become more flexible, agile, and customer focused.

In an e-commerce world, fulfillment strategies are evolving. The traditional model of shipping goods in bulk to brick-and-mortar stores is giving way to direct-to-consumer deliveries. This transition necessitates smaller, more frequent shipments and places a premium on speed and reliability. To meet these demands, businesses are experimenting with various strategies, including decentralizing distribution networks, employing advanced predictive analytics for efficient inventory management, and leveraging advanced technologies for quicker and more efficient order fulfillment.

Take, for example, Zara, the Spanish fast-fashion retailer. Zara's integrated online and offline retail strategy, combined with its advanced analytics and flexible supply chain, allows it to respond quickly to changing fashion trends. Their agile approach represents a stellar example of e-commerce-driven supply chain management.

Moreover, e-commerce has also brought about a paradigm shift in last-mile delivery - the final step in the delivery process where a product moves from a transportation hub to its destination. As e-commerce continues to grow, last-mile delivery services have become increasingly complex and critical. Consumers now demand fast, reliable, and often free deliveries, which requires highly efficient and flexible logistics networks.

Innovative solutions are emerging to tackle this challenge. Drone deliveries, smart lockers, and crowd-sourced delivery are a few examples of how companies are reimagining last-mile delivery. For instance, Amazon's Prime Air service aims to leverage drone technology to deliver packages within 30 minutes of order placement, representing a significant leap forward in delivery speed and efficiency.

Furthermore, e-commerce has necessitated a dramatic rethinking of return logistics. With e-commerce, the rate of returns is significantly higher compared to traditional brick-and-mortar retail. This creates the need for efficient reverse logistics processes to handle returns and exchanges quickly and cost-effectively. Technology plays a critical role here too, with solutions ranging from AI-powered quality checks to automated sorting and restocking.

Lastly, it is crucial to mention the growing importance of sustainability in e-commerce. As consumers become increasingly conscious of their environmental footprint, businesses are under pressure to adopt eco-friendly practices. This need extends across the supply chain – from sustainable packaging to carbon-neutral delivery options. Companies like Etsy, a global marketplace for handmade goods and vintage items, have committed to offsetting 100% of carbon emissions generated by shipping.

As we dive deeper into the future of supply chain management, the influence of e-commerce is impossible to ignore. It's a powerful force driving the transformation of traditional supply chains into highly responsive, customer-centric, and technology-driven systems. The challenge and opportunity for supply chain professionals lie in harnessing the potential of e-commerce and successfully integrating it into broader supply chain strategies. Navigating these changes effectively will be the key to success in the world of "Logistics 2040.

CHAPTER 9
ADVANCES IN MATERIAL HANDLING

As the pace of technological innovation quickens, every aspect of the supply chain experiences unprecedented transformation. One area where these changes are especially visible is material handling – a crucial part of warehouse and distribution center operations. In this chapter, we'll explore how robotics, automation, and future technologies are reshaping the world of material handling.

The advent of robotics in warehouse management is more than a futuristic concept – it's already a reality. The use of robots in warehouses has significantly increased in the past few years. They handle a variety of tasks, from pick and pack operations to sorting and transporting goods. Robots offer several advantages: they increase efficiency, reduce errors, and can operate around the clock.

Amazon Robotics, a subsidiary of the e-commerce giant, offers an excellent case study. Their robotic system uses automated guided vehicles to move shelves of goods to human workers, who then pick and pack orders. This system has reduced the time taken to pick an item from about an hour and a half to less than 15 minutes, demonstrating a remarkable increase in productivity.

Next in the automation frontier is Automated Storage and Retrieval Systems (AS/RS). These systems automatically place and retrieve items from specific locations, optimizing warehouse space utilization, and reducing labor requirements. AS/RS come in many forms, from fixed-aisle systems used in large-scale warehouses to goods-to-person systems ideal for smaller spaces. The central promise is a more efficient, scalable, and error-free system of inventory management.

A good example of AS/RS implementation is the Adidas "Speed factory." In these fully automated factories, AS/RS systems manage materials, and robotic arms handle assembly, producing a pair of shoes every 30 seconds. While these factories represent the upper echelons of automation, they signify what the future of warehousing could look like.

Beyond robotics and AS/RS, a slew of innovations are on the horizon for material handling technologies. Take, for instance, the use of Augmented Reality (AR) for order picking. AR devices can display picking instructions directly into workers' fields of view, helping them locate items more quickly and reducing errors.

Also noteworthy is the development of the Internet of Things (IoT) and AI in predictive maintenance for material handling equipment. Sensors collect data on machine operations, which AI algorithms then analyze to predict when a machine might fail. This allows for timely maintenance, preventing costly downtime.

Another exciting development is the use of exoskeletons – wearable devices that can increase strength and endurance. These devices could assist workers in lifting heavy items, reducing the risk of injury, and increasing productivity.

It's important to mention that these technological advancements do not imply a reduction in the importance of human workers. Instead, the focus will shift from manual, repetitive tasks to more strategic roles, such as managing these systems, analyzing data they generate, and making strategic decisions based on these insights. Consequently, there will be an increased need for upskilling and training workers for these new roles. The transformation of material handling technologies embodies the larger shifts occurring within the logistics and supply chain industry. As technology continues to advance, businesses need to stay abreast of these developments and understand how to integrate them effectively. From robotics to AI, the future of material handling is increasingly automated, connected, and intelligent. The "Logistics 2040" landscape promises to be an exciting one, and material handling technology will be a key player in this future.

CHAPTER 10
THE FOURTH INDUSTRIAL REVOLUTION

The Fourth Industrial Revolution, or Industry 4.0, refers to the ongoing transformation of traditional manufacturing and industrial practices combined with the latest smart technology. This revolution has been characterized by the digitalization and interconnection of products, value chains, and business models, and has profound implications for supply chain and logistics.

The core principles of Industry 4.0 are interconnection, information transparency, technical assistance, and decentralized decisions. It integrates cyber-physical systems, Internet of Things (IoT), cloud computing, cognitive computing, and digital twins – each of which plays a significant role in revolutionizing the supply chain and logistics sector.

Cyber-physical systems (CPS), the backbone of Industry 4.0, are integrations of computation, networking, and physical processes. Embedded computers and networks monitor and control the physical processes, with feedback loops where physical processes affect computations and vice versa. In supply chains, CPS will allow organizations to control physical assets digitally, providing the opportunity to build and manage fully integrated, collaborative systems that respond in real time to changing demands or conditions in the factory, in the supply network, and in customer needs. This leads to increased visibility, better quality control, improved productivity, and enhanced efficiency.

For example, BMW's assembly system is now so flexible that the same line can simultaneously produce a variety of models, based on real-time demand inputs, resulting in cost savings and responsiveness to market demand. Such "smart" factories, products, and networks are the reality in leading firms today.

Among the various advancements of Industry 4.0, the role of 'Digital Twins' stands out as a game changer for supply chain planning. A digital twin is a virtual replica of a product, process, or system that can be used for testing, optimization, and maintenance. In the context of supply chain management, a digital twin of the supply chain can provide an accurate, comprehensive, and dynamic representation of the system, allowing for improved monitoring, analysis, and optimization.

Consider an example of General Electric (GE), which has created digital twins for tens of thousands of its jet engines currently in service. These digital twins enable GE to predict maintenance accurately before an issue occurs, reducing downtime and optimizing the maintenance process.

In the supply chain context, digital twins enable organizations to model their supply chains, run simulations and 'what-if' scenarios, and predict outcomes based on varying factors. They can be used to analyze the impact of a new product launch, changes in trade regulations, or disruptions like a supplier going out of business or a natural disaster impacting a warehouse.

Digital twins are also crucial for integrating and optimizing end-to-end supply chain processes – from demand planning and production scheduling to logistics and delivery. This results in a supply chain that is not just interconnected, but truly synchronized – an essential attribute in the fast-paced, demand-driven market landscape of the future.

The implications of Industry 4.0 on supply chain and logistics are vast. As we move towards a more interconnected and digital world, companies need to invest in advanced technologies, upskill their workforce, and develop strategies that can leverage these technologies. This transition may be challenging, but the potential benefits — improved efficiency, agility, customer responsiveness, and ultimately, competitive advantage — are significant.

In the coming chapters, we will continue exploring more elements shaping the "Logistics 2040" landscape, providing insights into how these trends are changing the way we think about and manage supply chains.

CHAPTER 11
THE POWER OF PREDICTIVE ANALYTICS AND ARTIFICIAL INTELLIGENCE IN SUPPLY CHAIN

The role of predictive analytics in supply chain management cannot be understated. As global supply chains become increasingly complex and fraught with uncertainties, predictive analytics have become critical for successful supply chain planning and management. This chapter explores how predictive analytics, scenario modeling, and artificial intelligence (AI) are shaping the future of supply chain planning.

Predictive analytics involves the use of data, statistical algorithms, and machine learning techniques to identify future outcomes based on historical data. In the context of supply chains, predictive analytics can provide insights into future demand, supply disruptions, logistical challenges, and more.

For instance, using predictive analytics, a retailer could anticipate consumer demand for different products at different times of the year and plan inventory accordingly. Additionally, companies can predict potential supply chain disruptions—such as supplier bankruptcies or transport delays—and create contingency plans.

Scenario modeling is an excellent tool that works hand in hand with predictive analytics. It allows supply chain managers to create and analyze different 'what-if' situations to prepare for multiple eventualities. For example, scenario modeling could help a company prepare for potential increases in tariffs or changes in exchange rates, assessing the impacts of different strategies on the supply chain's resilience and the company's bottom line.

AI is revolutionizing the field of demand forecasting and inventory optimization. Traditional forecasting methods often rely on historical sales data, but AI can analyze a vast array of factors—including market trends, economic indicators, weather patterns, and social media sentiment—to create more accurate demand forecasts.

For instance, IBM's AI-driven tool Watson uses machine learning algorithms to analyze both structured data—like sales history, product information, and industry reports—and unstructured data—like weather information, social media feeds, and news articles—to predict demand with unprecedented accuracy.

In terms of inventory optimization, AI can help companies strike the right balance between carrying too much inventory (which ties up capital and risks obsolescence) and carrying too little (which can lead to stock-outs and lost sales). Using AI, companies can dynamically adjust safety stock levels based on predicted demand variability, lead times, and service level targets.

AI and predictive analytics also play a significant role in creating a demand-driven supply chain. This means moving away from a supply-focused push model—where products are produced in large quantities and pushed through the supply chain—to a customer-focused pull model—where production is closely aligned with real-time customer demand.

In the next chapter, we will delve deeper into the integration of technology in supply chain management, including blockchain, the Internet of Things, and more.

CHAPTER 12
REVOLUTIONIZING GLOBAL SOURCING THROUGH TECHNOLOGY AND EFFECTIVE RISK MANAGEMENT

Global sourcing, the practice of sourcing goods and services across geopolitical boundaries, has become an integral part of the supply chain strategy of many businesses. While it has brought about significant benefits, such as cost savings, increased efficiency, and access to new markets, it also poses a new set of challenges, including increased complexity, cultural differences, legal considerations, and heightened risk exposure. This chapter explores the latest trends in global sourcing, the use of technology for efficient procurement, and essential risk management strategies.

The world of global sourcing is constantly evolving as companies adapt to shifting economic landscapes, geopolitical developments, and technological advancements. A rising trend is the shift towards ethical sourcing, with increased consumer demand for transparency and sustainability driving companies to ensure their supply chains align with environmental and social standards.

Companies are also diversifying their supplier base to mitigate risks and ensure a stable supply chain. This often means sourcing from different countries or regions to avoid overdependence on a single source. This strategy has been particularly crucial in light of the recent disruptions caused by the COVID-19 pandemic and ongoing geopolitical tensions.

Technology has been a game-changer in procurement, ushering in new efficiencies and capabilities. Procurement software platforms have streamlined procurement processes, reducing manual tasks, improving accuracy, and enabling real-time tracking and reporting. Such platforms can automate everything from supplier selection to contract management, ensuring a seamless and efficient procurement process.

Emerging technologies like AI and machine learning are also being leveraged to enhance procurement. For instance, AI can analyze vast amounts of data to predict supplier performance, market trends, and even foresee potential supply disruptions. This enables companies to make data-driven decisions and manage their supply chain proactively.

Blockchain, another transformative technology, brings about increased transparency and security in procurement. It provides a tamper-proof, decentralized record of transactions, ensuring traceability and accountability in the supply chain.

Risk management in global sourcing is paramount. Companies must identify, assess, and mitigate various risks, including supply disruptions, currency fluctuations, and compliance issues. This process involves a deep understanding of the sourcing environment, thorough supplier evaluations, and regular audits.

Moreover, companies are implementing supply chain risk management software that allows for real-time risk assessment and mitigation. These platforms can monitor a range of risk indicators, from political instability and natural disasters to supplier financial health, enabling companies to react swiftly to potential disruptions.

In essence, while global sourcing offers remarkable opportunities, it also comes with a complex set of challenges. Leveraging technology and implementing robust risk management strategies are crucial for companies to navigate this complexity and achieve success in the global sourcing arena. As we move forward, the trend towards digitalization and risk diversification will continue to shape the landscape of global sourcing. In the upcoming chapter, we will explore the future of sustainable supply chains, discussing how businesses are rising to the challenge of environmental responsibility in their supply chain operations.

Chapter 13
The New Horizon of Freight Transportation: Autonomous Vehicles, Digital Brokerage, and the Future of Air, Sea, and Rail Freight

Freight transportation has been an indispensable component of the global supply chain, playing a crucial role in linking producers and consumers. Yet, the traditional freight industry has been characterized by inefficiencies, environmental concerns, and safety issues. Today, with the advent of technological innovations, the landscape of freight transportation is experiencing a significant shift. This chapter focuses on the rise of autonomous vehicles in freight transportation, the emergence of digital freight brokerage, and the prospective future of air, sea, and rail freight.

Autonomous vehicles have transitioned from science fiction to reality in recent years, with numerous pilot programs showcasing their potential in freight transportation. Self-driving trucks promise to transform road freight by increasing efficiency, reducing accidents caused by driver fatigue, and addressing the chronic shortage of truck drivers. Despite regulatory challenges and technical hurdles, companies like Tesla, Waymo, and Embark are heavily investing in this technology, signifying a promising future.

Digital freight brokerage, another groundbreaking trend, is revolutionizing the way shippers connect with carriers. These platforms leverage artificial intelligence and machine learning to match shippers and carriers based on various factors like route, price, and capacity, eliminating the need for traditional brokers. This not only streamlines the process but also increases transparency, reduces costs, and improves service reliability. Companies like Convoy, Uber Freight, and Loadsmart are leading the way in this digital transformation.

As we look towards the future of air, sea, and rail freight, several trends and innovations emerge. For air freight, the use of drones for small parcel delivery is on the rise, particularly for last-mile delivery in remote areas. On the other hand, larger cargo planes are becoming more fuel-efficient and environmentally friendly.

In sea freight, the focus is on green shipping practices. New emission regulations have propelled the industry towards cleaner fuels and energy-efficient technologies. Furthermore, autonomous ships and digital twins of vessels are no longer a distant reality, with the potential to increase efficiency and safety.

Meanwhile, rail freight is experiencing a resurgence, primarily due to its cost-effectiveness and lower environmental impact compared to other transport modes. Railroads are increasingly automated and digitized, enhancing efficiency and visibility. Innovative concepts like hyperloop also propose a transformative change in freight (and passenger) rail transport, offering high-speed, energy-efficient alternatives.

As we navigate through the logistics 2040 landscape, the freight industry must continue to innovate and adapt. The integration of cutting-edge technology is no longer a luxury but a necessity for surviving and thriving in this fast-evolving industry. In the next chapter, we delve into the world of sustainable supply chains, a concept that is rapidly moving from a 'nice-to-have' to a 'must-have' in the logistics realm.

Chapter 14
The Future of Business Models in Logistics: Platform-Based Operations, Sharing Economy, and Subscription Services

The world of business has been fundamentally reshaped by the advent of the digital age. Business models that were once staples of the industry are being gradually supplanted by innovative concepts designed to leverage the capabilities of advanced technologies and cater to the evolving demands of the market. In this chapter, we delve into the rise of platform-based business models in logistics, the implications of the sharing economy, and the emergence of subscription models in the context of demand-driven supply chains.

Platform-based business models have surged in popularity across a multitude of industries, with logistics being no exception. At the heart of this model is a digital platform that connects various users, facilitating interactions that deliver value. For logistics, these platforms connect shippers and carriers, and sometimes even end consumers, leveraging AI and data analytics to optimize routes, match capacities, and streamline the entire shipping process. Companies like Flexport and Convoy are prime examples of the rise of platform-based logistics.

The sharing economy has also found its place in the logistics industry. Traditionally, the logistics sector was dominated by asset-heavy companies. However, this has changed with the emergence of asset-light business models, where firms leverage resources owned by others. Much like Uber or Airbnb in their respective industries, companies such as Uber Freight and Flexe are redefining logistics by facilitating the sharing of transportation and warehousing capacities. This not only allows for better capacity utilization but also promotes a more flexible and scalable logistics operation.

Subscription models, popularized by companies like Netflix and Spotify, are beginning to make their mark on logistics, particularly within the scope of demand-driven supply chains. As e-commerce continues to thrive, businesses are seeking ways to secure customer loyalty and predict demand more accurately. Subscription models offer a solution, providing a steady stream of predictable orders and enabling companies to better plan their logistics operations. Companies like Blue Apron and Amazon Prime are notable examples, leveraging subscription models to drive their logistics operations.

These evolving business models offer promising benefits but come with their own set of challenges, ranging from regulatory concerns to issues with customer trust and data security. For logistics firms to successfully adopt these models, they must be willing to navigate these challenges and continuously adapt to the changing business landscape.

Looking forward, as the digital transformation continues to unfold, logistics companies should prepare for more disruptive changes. Keeping pace with these changes will not be easy but will be essential for survival and growth in the era of Logistics 2040. In the next chapter, we discuss the importance of environmental sustainability in logistics and supply chain management - a responsibility and challenge that businesses of the future cannot afford to ignore.

Chapter 15
Urban Logistics: Challenges, Innovations, and the Role of Smart Cities

As urban populations swell and city dwellers demand ever-faster deliveries, the urban logistics landscape faces unprecedented challenges. The complexities associated with high-density living, congested traffic, and strict environmental regulations necessitate the development of innovative solutions in last-mile delivery, and a new way of envisioning cities – as intelligent, connected, and designed with logistics in mind.

Urban logistics presents a multitude of challenges. Traffic congestion, caused by an increasing number of delivery vehicles on the road, not only slows delivery times but also contributes to urban pollution. Limited access to delivery points in inner-city areas, particularly during peak hours, further exacerbates the problem. Compounding these issues, the pressure to meet the 'same-day delivery' expectation requires logistics companies to re-evaluate their traditional supply chain strategies.

To mitigate these challenges, companies have been exploring various innovative solutions. Micro-fulfillment centers, strategically located within urban areas, serve as mini distribution hubs that can expedite last-mile delivery. Drone deliveries, though still in the experimental phase in many places, offer a promising, albeit controversial, solution to bypass traffic congestion. Meanwhile, the deployment of electric delivery vehicles and cargo bikes can address environmental concerns. Companies such as Amazon and DHL have been at the forefront of implementing these innovations.

Enter 'smart cities' – urban environments where traditional networks and services are made more efficient with the use of digital and telecommunication technologies. As more cities begin their transformation into smart cities, the impact on logistics is significant.

IoT (Internet of Things) sensors can provide real-time traffic data, allowing delivery vehicles to take the most efficient routes. Intelligent traffic management systems can dynamically adjust traffic signals based on traffic volume and congestion, improving traffic flow. Moreover, shared data platforms can facilitate the coordination of deliveries, reducing the number of vehicles on the road.

Moreover, the integration of urban planning and logistics, where logistics considerations are taken into account when designing city infrastructure, can further optimize urban logistics. This includes the design of delivery-friendly buildings with dedicated delivery and storage spaces and the planning of urban consolidation centers, where goods can be combined for efficient delivery.

In conclusion, the challenges of urban logistics demand forward-thinking solutions and the leveraging of advanced technologies. As we navigate the future towards Logistics 2040, the successful integration of logistics into urban life will require close collaboration between city planners, logistics providers, technology developers, and regulators.

In the next chapter, we will delve into another key aspect of future logistics – environmental sustainability. We will look at the critical role of green logistics, how to measure and reduce carbon footprints, and the importance of circular economy principles in the logistics sector.

Chapter 16
The Future of Cold Chain Logistics: Trends, Technologies, and Case Studies

In an increasingly globalized world, the temperature-controlled supply chain, also known as the cold chain, plays a critical role in ensuring the safe and timely transportation of temperature-sensitive products like food, pharmaceuticals, and certain high-tech equipment. As we march towards 2040, this chapter focuses on the emerging trends, the role of technology in maintaining product integrity, and lessons we can learn from companies leading in cold chain logistics.

Future trends in the cold chain industry are driven by a combination of regulatory changes, customer expectations, and technological advancements. Regulatory changes, particularly those aimed at ensuring product safety and reducing environmental impact, are forcing companies to upgrade their cold chain practices. Customer expectations for faster delivery and complete transparency are pushing companies to innovate and adapt. Simultaneously, breakthrough technologies offer new opportunities for companies to enhance their cold chain logistics.

Technology plays an indispensable role in maintaining product integrity. Innovations such as IoT sensors, real-time tracking, and advanced packaging solutions are all transforming how companies handle temperature-sensitive products.

IoT sensors and real-time monitoring devices can track a product's condition, including temperature, humidity, and even shock, throughout the supply chain journey. With advanced data analytics, any deviation from predefined conditions can trigger immediate corrective actions, significantly reducing the risk of product loss.

Moreover, developments in packaging technology, such as phase-change materials (PCMs) and vacuum insulated panels (VIPs), are improving insulation and extending the duration that products can stay within their required temperature ranges. This is particularly crucial in the transportation of life-saving pharmaceuticals, like vaccines, where maintaining product integrity can literally mean the difference between life and death.

Next, let's explore some companies that have excelled in leveraging technology to manage their cold chains effectively.

Consider the case of Maersk, the global shipping giant. In response to stricter regulations and a commitment to reduce food wastage, Maersk has pioneered the use of remote container management (RCM) systems. This technology allows the company to monitor the condition of its refrigerated containers in real-time, using data to optimize operations and minimize losses.

In the pharmaceutical industry, companies like Pfizer and Moderna have been commended for their efficient cold chain management during the COVID-19 pandemic. Their vaccines, which required ultra-low temperatures during transportation, presented immense cold chain challenges. Through advanced packaging, IoT technology, and collaboration with logistics partners, they were able to deliver billions of doses worldwide, demonstrating the value of efficient cold chain logistics.

As we look ahead to Logistics 2040, the importance of the cold chain can only increase. Whether it's delivering fresh groceries, transporting lab-grown meat, or ensuring the safe arrival of next-generation medicines, mastering the complexities of the cold chain will be key to success in an ever-more-connected world.

In the upcoming chapter, we will explore the critical importance of sustainability in logistics and the strategies companies can adopt to reduce their environmental impact while maintaining efficiency and competitiveness.

Chapter 17
Strengthening Supply Chain Security: The Role of Technology, Cybersecurity Risks, and Resilience Strategies

As supply chains continue to grow in complexity and extend across borders, so does their exposure to a wide range of risks. From cyberattacks and data breaches to theft and sabotage, supply chain security has become a top priority. This chapter delves into the role of technology in enhancing supply chain security, the potential cybersecurity risks of digital supply chains, and strategies for building secure, resilient supply chains.

Technology plays a dual role when it comes to supply chain security. On one hand, it can expose supply chains to new vulnerabilities, and on the other, it provides powerful tools for enhancing security.

Technologies such as blockchain, IoT, AI, and machine learning can significantly improve the security of supply chains. Blockchain technology, with its secure, decentralized, and immutable features, offers traceability and transparency, making it difficult for unauthorized changes to be made without detection. IoT devices can provide real-time tracking of goods, mitigating the risk of theft or misplacement. AI and machine learning can identify patterns and anomalies in large data sets, providing early warning of potential security breaches.

However, the increasing digitization of supply chains opens new avenues for cyberattacks. With sensitive data flowing between suppliers, manufacturers, and consumers, supply chains can become a prime target for cybercriminals. Cybersecurity risks in digital supply chains include data breaches, ransomware attacks, and disruption of operations.

Building a secure and resilient supply chain requires a multi-layered strategy. This includes adopting robust cybersecurity measures, regular risk assessments, collaboration with partners, and creating a culture of security awareness.

Robust cybersecurity measures include encrypting sensitive data, implementing secure authentication protocols, regular patching and updating of software, and investing in cybersecurity tools like firewalls and intrusion detection systems.

Regular risk assessments can help identify potential vulnerabilities and threats, and help organizations develop mitigation strategies.

Collaboration with partners is critical, as a chain is only as strong as its weakest link. Sharing threat intelligence, best practices, and coordinating response strategies can greatly enhance overall supply chain security.

Finally, creating a culture of security awareness is a crucial component of any cybersecurity strategy. Employees at all levels need to be trained in secure practices, such as recognizing phishing attempts, using strong passwords, and reporting suspicious activity.

Security is not a one-time effort but an ongoing process that must adapt to the evolving threat landscape. Looking forward, the importance of supply chain security will only increase as businesses become more interconnected and reliant on digital technologies.

In the next chapter, we will dive deeper into the topic of sustainability in supply chains, examining its importance, challenges, and potential strategies for building sustainable, resilient supply chains.

Chapter 18
Customer Satisfaction, Technological Leverage, and Supplier Relationships in a Digital World

The rapid evolution of supply chain operations in the digital age has amplified the role of customer satisfaction, technology, and supplier relationships. This chapter will delve into how these aspects are interlinked, contributing to the overall efficiency and competitiveness of supply chains.

Supply chain operations have a direct and substantial impact on customer satisfaction. The fulfillment speed, accuracy of delivery, product availability, and responsiveness to changes or issues are just some of the supply chain factors that can make or break a customer's experience. A seamless supply chain that meets or exceeds customer expectations can be a crucial differentiator in today's competitive marketplace. Conversely, a hiccup in the supply chain – such as delayed delivery or stock-outs – can significantly damage customer satisfaction and brand reputation.

Technology can serve as a vital enabler in elevating the customer experience. For instance, advanced analytics and AI can provide insights into customer behavior, allowing businesses to forecast demand more accurately and reduce stock-outs or overstocks. Real-time tracking technologies can provide customers with visibility into their order status, increasing their sense of control and satisfaction. AI-driven chatbots and virtual assistants can provide round-the-clock customer service, resolving issues swiftly and efficiently.

In the digital world, maintaining and enhancing supplier relationships has its unique set of challenges and opportunities. On one hand, the proliferation of digital communication channels can lead to more frequent and transparent communication with suppliers. Supplier Relationship Management (SRM) systems can streamline interactions, making them more efficient and productive.

On the other hand, the increasing complexity of digital supply chains, coupled with the risks related to data security and privacy, calls for a heightened focus on building trust and ensuring compliance. It's essential to set clear expectations about data sharing, security, and performance metrics. Regular audits can help ensure compliance with these standards.

In summary, in an era where the customer is king, companies must leverage advanced technologies to meet the escalating customer expectations. Furthermore, as supply chains expand in a digital ecosystem, building and maintaining robust supplier relationships is more critical than ever. In the next chapter, we will discuss the future of logistics, its potential challenges, and the strategies that businesses can employ to stay ahead of the curve.

Chapter 19
Emerging Markets: The New Frontiers in Global Supply Chains

In the ever-evolving landscape of supply chain management, emerging markets have become increasingly significant. These markets, often characterized by rapid economic growth and industrialization, provide both opportunities and challenges for global supply chains. This chapter will delve into the role of these markets, the unique difficulties they pose, the potential benefits they offer, and real-world examples of successful supply chain operations within them.

Emerging markets, including regions such as Southeast Asia, Africa, Latin America, and parts of Eastern Europe, have started to play a critical role in global supply chains. Many factors contribute to this trend: their large and growing consumer bases, increasing purchasing power, vast labor pools, and often less saturated markets. From manufacturing to retail, these markets have become integral parts of global supply chain networks, either as sourcing destinations, manufacturing hubs, or growing consumer markets.

However, navigating emerging markets isn't without its challenges. Infrastructure is often less developed, which can pose significant logistics hurdles. Inconsistent regulatory environments and political instability can also create risks. Cultural differences can impact business operations and require adaptations in strategies.

Despite these hurdles, the potential for growth and competitive advantage in emerging markets is vast. Companies that can adapt to these markets, navigate their challenges, and tap into their potential can reap substantial rewards.

Let's look at a couple of case studies:

1.   Unilever in India: Unilever's operations in India offer an excellent example of a successful supply chain in an emerging market. The company tailored its supply chain strategy to accommodate India's diverse, vast, and primarily rural consumer base. It developed a multi-tier distribution model, leveraging local distributors and small retail shops to reach the most remote consumers. This flexible and localized approach has made Unilever one of the leading FMCG companies in India.

2.   Huawei in Africa: Chinese telecom giant Huawei has significantly invested in Africa, setting up an extensive supply chain for its products across the continent. It worked around infrastructural deficiencies by creating local assembly plants, reducing the need for extensive transportation. Additionally, it trained local workers, creating jobs and

helping it navigate cultural and regulatory landscapes.

While the challenges in emerging markets are significant, so too are the opportunities. The key lies in understanding these markets, adapting strategies to local conditions, building resilient and flexible supply chains, and ultimately, being patient as these markets mature. As we look towards 2040, companies that can achieve this will be well-positioned to lead in the global supply chain landscape.

Chapter 20
Beyond 2040: Charting the Course of Future Supply Chains

As we stand at the cusp of a new era in supply chain management, it is crucial to cast our gaze beyond the immediate future. The changes we've examined throughout this book will continue to evolve, leading to new paradigms that we can only begin to imagine. This final chapter aims to speculate on these far-future trends, discuss strategies for future-proofing supply chains, and evaluate the future of supply chain education and careers.

1. Predicting trends beyond 2040: Predicting the long-term future is always fraught with uncertainties. However, some clear trends are emerging. We can expect further integration of AI and machine learning, leading to unprecedented levels of automation. As technology continues to advance, we may see the rise of fully autonomous global supply networks that operate with minimal human intervention. The application of technologies like quantum computing could revolutionize how we handle vast amounts of data. Moreover, as sustainability becomes a global priority, we will see more 'green' supply chains, with an emphasis on circular economies and zero-waste operations.

2. Preparing supply chains for uncertainties: The supply chains of the future will need to be robust, resilient, and adaptable to thrive amidst uncertainties. Businesses will need to create redundancy, improve visibility across the supply chain, and invest in technology that allows for real-time monitoring and rapid response. Scenario planning and stress testing will become standard practices. Furthermore, building strong relationships with suppliers and customers will be crucial for sharing risk and improving overall supply chain resilience.

3. The future of supply chain education and careers: The supply chain professionals of the future will need to be technologically savvy, adaptable, and comfortable with constant change. They will need to understand advanced analytics, AI, and other emerging technologies. Consequently, supply chain education will have to evolve to meet these demands. More courses will integrate technology training, critical thinking, and strategy. As supply chains become more critical for businesses, we will see a continued demand for skilled supply chain professionals. At the same time, the rise of AI could see a shift in the types of jobs available, with more emphasis on overseeing and managing AI systems rather than performing routine tasks.

The future of supply chains beyond 2040 is speculative, it will be characterized by rapid technological advancement, a heightened focus on resilience, and an ever-increasing emphasis on sustainability. It is an exciting time for those in the field, with numerous opportunities for those willing to adapt and innovate. As we move towards this future, we must remember that the core goal remains the same: to deliver the right product, at the right time, in the right place, in the most efficient and sustainable way possible.

Conclusion
The Road Ahead for Supply Chain Management

As we draw this discourse to a close, we have traversed an enlightening journey, peeking into the rapidly approaching future of supply chain management. The vistas of change, powered by technological advancements, global dynamics, and shifting business priorities, promise a fascinating evolution in the way we manage and navigate supply chains.

1.   Recap of future trends and technologies: We have delved deep into the potential of AI and machine learning, heralding a new era of predictive analytics and data-driven decision-making. We've explored the rise of cyber-physical systems and Industry 4.0, unlocking unprecedented levels of automation and visibility. We've considered the transformative potential of digital twins, autonomous vehicles, smart warehousing, and advanced robotics. And throughout, we have underlined the increasing centrality of sustainability, cybersecurity, and resilience in tomorrow's supply chains.

2.   The strategic importance of supply chain management: What has emerged is a compelling picture of supply chain management not just as an operational function, but as a strategic cornerstone of business success. More than ever, supply chains are the arteries that keep the lifeblood of commerce flowing, connecting markets, products, and people in a global dance of creation, consumption, and competition. The ability to effectively manage these intricate networks will differentiate the leaders from the laggards, and the winners from the also-rans.

3.   Final thoughts and inspiration: To the next generation of supply chain professionals, the road ahead is both daunting and exhilarating. You will be tasked with managing complexity, uncertainty, and change on a scale unprecedented in human history. But the opportunities for innovation, impact, and leadership are vast.

Remember, supply chain management is not just about moving products. It's about connecting people and societies, shaping sustainable and equitable economies, and building a future that works for all. The technologies and trends we have discussed are mere tools. The real power lies in your hands. It is your creativity, your values, and your leadership that will shape the supply chains of the future.

As we navigate towards 2040 and beyond, let us remember that in every challenge lies an opportunity, and in every shift, the chance to redefine the status quo. We hope this book has equipped you with knowledge and provoked thoughts for the journey ahead. The future of supply chain management is not set in stone; it is yours to shape.

With every link we forge in the chain, let us strive to make a difference, driving not just operational efficiency, but social progress, environmental sustainability, and shared prosperity. Welcome to the future of supply chain management. It promises to be a thrilling ride.

Glossary

1.   **Artificial Intelligence (AI):** A branch of computer science that simulates human intelligence in machines programmed to "think" like a human and mimic their actions.

2.   **Autonomous Vehicles:** Vehicles capable of sensing their environment and operating without human involvement.

3.   **Big Data:** Extremely large data sets that can be analyzed computationally to reveal patterns, trends, and associations, especially relating to human behavior and interactions.

4.   **Cyber-Physical Systems (CPS):** Systems that integrate computational, networking, and physical processes. Embedded computers and networks monitor and control the physical processes, with feedback loops where physical processes affect computations and vice versa.

5.   **Cybersecurity:** The protection of computer systems and networks from information disclosure, theft of, or damage to their hardware, software, or electronic data, as well as from the disruption or misdirection of the services they provide.

6.   **Digital Freight Brokerage:** A service that uses web-based platforms to connect shippers and carriers for freight transportation.

7.   **Digital Twins:** A digital replica of a physical entity, process, or system, which can be used for various purposes like testing, simulation, and optimization.

8.   **Industry 4.0:** The current trend of automation and data exchange in manufacturing technologies. It includes cyber-physical systems, the Internet of things, cloud computing, and cognitive computing.

9.   **Last-mile Delivery:** The movement of goods from a transportation hub to the final delivery destination, typically a personal residence, which is the final leg of delivery.

10. **Machine Learning:** A type of artificial intelligence that allows software applications to become more accurate in predicting outcomes without being explicitly programmed to do so.

11. **Predictive Analytics:** The use of data, statistical algorithms, and machine learning techniques to identify the likelihood of future outcomes based on historical data.

12. **Real-Time Analytics:** The analysis and reporting of data as soon as it enters the system.

13. **Scenario Modeling:** A process of creating multiple, detailed outlines of what could happen in various risk situations.

14. **Smart Warehousing:** The use of advanced technologies such as

AI, robotics, IoT, and cloud computing in a warehouse to improve efficiency, accuracy, and speed.

15. **Supply Chain:** A network between a company and its suppliers to produce and distribute a specific product to the final buyer. It represents the steps to get a product or service from its original state to the customer.

16. **Supply Chain Management:** The management of the flow of goods and services, involving the movement and storage of raw materials, of work-in-process inventory, and of finished goods from point of origin to point of consumption.

17. **Supply Chain Visibility:** The ability of stakeholders throughout the supply chain to access real-time data related to the order process, inventory, delivery, and potential supply chain disruptions.

18. **Sustainability:** The ability to maintain certain processes or states at a certain level for the long term, often with a strong emphasis on environmental, social, and economic aspects.

19. **3PLs and 4PLs:** Third-party logistics (3PL) providers offer outsourced logistics services, which encompass anything that involves the management of one or more facets of procurement and fulfillment activities. Fourth-party logistics (4PL) providers have a broad reach within a company's supply chain and offer strategic insight and management over the supply chain.

20. **Urban Logistics:** The process of optimizing logistics and transport activities in urban areas while considering the social, environmental, economic, and technological impacts.

These terms, among others, form the crux of the discussions in this book, serving as the foundation of our journey into the future of supply chain management.

ABOUT THE AUTHOR

"Logistics 2040: Navigating the Future of Supply Chain Management" brings a unique and deeply insightful perspective to the subject, enriched by 15 years of hands-on experience in the Marine Corps logistics Operation. A seasoned expert in the field, the author served in various key logistical roles within the military, where precision, efficiency, and adaptability were paramount.

www.ingramcontent.com/pod-product-compliance
Lightning Source LLC
Chambersburg PA
CBHW062301290526
45794CB00006B/2648